Against Myself

Lou Pépin Poussard

BookLeaf Publishing

Presentation by *BookLeaf Publishing*

Web: www.bookleafpub.com

E-mail: info@bookleafpub.com

ISBN: 978-93-95755-21-4

First edition 2022

*To my mother, maman, mumma bear, always
supporting any of my crazy projects.*

*To my brothers, who grew taller and stronger
than me.*

To all these people who told me I could write.

Ελεος

All in compassion she stands,
Forgiving, with Clemence and Mercy
She is well

Poison

Drowning in all this good will
Giving her all, unable to stop,
Unworthy or not of her aid

Sinking

Held down by the ones she helped
Held down by the promises made
Tied up in a great knot

Drowning

In the trap she made for herself
One by one selected threads
Against her Nature, she cuts

Freed

If my speech is of silver my silence is of gold

If the morning sigh coming from my lips, could be written as a Speech, words would not fail me anymore. That is, if only my eyes were to be muted. As, of their talk, my thoughts can be read, far too easily. Those treacherous silver eyes of mine. my ears, deaf from all those heavy days of silence, could hear again. This is, if only your lips, were the one to whisper in them. of all felonies, the most dreaded, is to play pretend, convinced that those gold coated words, are worth all the stone thrown.

If the morning sigh coming from
my lips, could be written as a
Speech, words would not fail me anymore. That
is, if only my eyes were to be muted. As,
of their talk, my thoughts can be read, far too
easily. Those treacherous
silver eyes of mine.

my ears, deaf from all those heavy days of
silence, could hear again. This
is, if only your lips, were the one to whisper in
them.

of all felonies, the most dreaded, is to play
pretend, convinced that those
gold coated words, are worth all the stone
thrown.

Irony

And it is when all is fine
That I sink

When this time I was smiling
My eyes misted
My lips started trembling
And tears rolled down my cheeks

And that's when everything goes wrong
That I smile

Still

All was once dark
Now all around was bright
from Her embrace I was now far.
"Even Death did not want me around."

The Cliff

Years pass by
Still you stay, immutable

Glimpse of a cliff
Dignified in all time and weather
As if the Ocean and its claws
On You had no effect

Strong
Your children protecting,
Neither Men nor Nature will reach
Them had you decided this way

You
Still
Won't
Budge

But
The Cliff one day
Will collapse
As the others, undermined by the Ocean's
scheme
And all the houses she sheltered
Will sink

Although
Their inhabitants
Will live on
Having grown
Stronger from the teaching
Of their life along the Cliff

To Find

Find the strength
To get up again
    To fight for yourself
        To love yourself

Find the strength
To learn
    To understand
        To explain

Find the strength
To get up, once again
    To smile
        To pretend

Find the strength

But I wanted just
    To not find strength
                but happiness.

My Life

One might say
My life is not
So bad
So sad
But imagine
What it feels like
In the deph of one's despair
To be told those words
When no light
no love
no laugh
as sincere as they can be
Can reach you

These Kids

As both nonsense and truth
came out of their mouths.
I got better

That's when Romie explained
The biggest:
"He is bigger
than the small
and the big."
and I laughed

That's when Elisa whispered
"You know when we're adult
we can't always have a prince charming.
not always"
And a tear rolled down my cheek

That's when Valence shouted
"You know
my daddy's name
is Untie!"
And I got confused

That's when Brune giggled
"He can't be wet,

he doesn't have hair!"
And I laughed too

That's when Alix asked
"What is excellent?"
And after I explained he said
"Me I say you are excellent!"

As both truth and nonsense
came out of these kids' mouths
I decided to continue living.

Artemis

Appollo and Artemis
Equal balance of sun and moon
Nature gave two and two were gained
None of them I chose
But all now dear to heart
As Apollo were by blood linked
Now for Artemis,
No less important,
Blood can be shed,
Earth can de destroyed
Unleashed be the Hounds of Hell,
If they were to be wounded
Body or Soul.

To Someone Worth it

As the photographs fade, I remember

From time to time, I need You
Your familiar embrace as I get Home,
Your overwhelming, annoying, precious
presence

Our life paths are not the same,
Yours is not to be tempered by mine.
I believe soul and Mind
In the person You were, are and will be.

You grew taller, You grew smarter, You grew
stronger
Still I will protect You. Always.
From time to time, You need me.

Burden

When caring falls onto the shoulders
And slowly becomes
a bittersweet burden
And their names are the only ones
filling our written wishes
Those wishes,
made for
us

Monosyllabic

Are you okay?

-Yes

How was your day?

-Fine

What are you doing today?

-Dunno

[I love you?

-I love you.]

Page Turner

Turn the page for good
When the content
Is not interesting anymore

Don't be dwell on too long
Start a new book
Even if you dearly loved the characters

Chaaltu

Their language, their smile, their open arms.
And it is when I learn about them that I realise
how much I don't know. How much could,
should and will be learned. How far from reality
I always have been, that my reality is not
everyone's, and mine is miles and miles and
miles from being the worst.
Crimson. Our flags only common colour. Blue
like those eyes on mine, white like my
–too—fair skin, crimson like my blood. Green
like the leaves on the trees of their country,
Yellow like the sun rising on their land, Crimson
like their blood, and a Star to protect us all.
Their language, their smile, their open arms.
Feeling as if I could recognise them in a crowd
full of unknown people, though I probably
would not. Their language, their smile, their
open arms. Unknown people, that is what they
are, I have never met them, I have never hugged
them. Even though, they gave me a name.
Chaaltu. "Above Anything". I don't know them;
I have never met them. They became a part of
me before I even had the chance to hug them.

Canva

Brushing   over fainted   colors
Blur rin g   it   all
dip pin g,   d ry in g
O n c e   a g a i n
No satis-   f a c t i o n
Brushing   o v e r
Out l i n e   F i ll i n g
F i n a l l y   Looking   like   s o m e t h i n g

Dancers

Their steps echoing
Fainted silhouettes above their heads
Moving along
All in Feathers and leather
As the breeze meets the warmth of the fireplace
All eyes turn to their unplanned performance

How wrong it was

How wrong was it of me to think
That he would be the one
To support me at any time

How wrong was it of her to think
That he would change back
To the one she used to love

How wrong was it of us to think
That he had an ounce of civility
Left for him to respect our choices

How wrong was it for them to pretend
That everything was fine
When they could see us suffering

How wrong was it?
Just how fast this family crumbled,
After years of pretending,

How right would it be
For them
To finally go their own way

Imaginary

Intentionally deceiving
Mocking the born-again butterflies
All words were said, none of them carried
meaning
Game of pretends; one in one's palm, one hidden
In pain came the answer
None of us ever admitted to our one true fear
All behind closed doors, behind curtains
Right to my enamoured eyes
You were lying

I grew to love tempests

By a most dreary night
after the wind awoke
after the clouds fought and cried
came competing
Lightning; electrifying, destroying
Thunder; loud and passing by
and Hail; heavy and feared
All performing together in Nature's most feared
symphony.

As the angry ocean threw it waves
crushing down onto the shore
Our windows suffered, cried for help
Praying for it to stop by midnight.
At the back of the house
a room, three young souls usually as
tempestuous as this night
Sharing this place for comfort and rest
Sleeping so tight not even the wind's fury could
awake
Waiting for dawn while dreaming at peace.

Reality

Out of their Cloudy Comfort
They witness the Great destruction
Of the World they thought would last

Brothers

Half across the globe
Mingling with others

The only time
I am close to this blood of mine

Caring for them as I
I left them at home

Writing them
This poem